Let's Meet Ms. Money

Written by Rich Grant

Printed in the United States of America
ISBN 978-1-64254-849-5

This book is dedicated to those parents and grandparents
who recognize the importance of including financial
literacy in the lives of our young people.

A special thanks to my children, Alexis, Jenna and Ricky,
who include family values in their lives.

Thank you to my grandchildren, Grant, Dominic, Nathan and Owen, who
inspired me to help them take this one step towards financial literacy.

Thank you to the most important person in my life, my wife.
Glenna has always allowed me to pursue my passions even
when it requires her to read and reread all my writings
and then read them again.

We can count to 100!

Good morning! My name is Ms. Money. I know you all can count numbers. Today you are going to learn what money looks like, how to count it, how and why we use money, and how we earn it.

Money is made either of metal or paper. Metal coins come in pennies, nickels, dimes and quarters.
This is what the coins look like:

Penny   1 cent

Nickel   5 cents

Dime   10 cents

Quarter   25 cents

Paper money includes a 1 dollar bill, a 5 dollar bill, a 10 dollar bill and a 20 dollar bill.

This is what paper money looks like:

Ms. Money wants to be sure you know your coins and bills. So, try to match the amount of money with the coin or bill.

Amount of Money   **Coin or Bill**

1 dollar bill ($1.00)

Quarter ($.25 cents)

20 dollar bill ($20.00)

Dime ($.10 cents)

Do you remember how you counted to 100? In the same way, Ms. Money wants you to count the value of the coins. So, let's count the money and see what we get.

Grant's Mom told us Grant had a penny, two quarters and a dime in his piggy bank.

Penny - 1 cent

Quarters - 25 cents

Dime - 10 cents

How much money does Grant have in his piggy bank?

Do you remember how you counted to 100? In the same way, Ms. Money wants you to count the value of the paper money. So, let's count the money and see what we get.

Dominic's Mom told us D received gifts of money from his grammy, his aunt and his father, for his birthday. He put the money in his piggy bank.

5 dollar bill ($5.00)

20 dollar bill ($20.00)

1 dollar bill ($1.00)

How much money does Dominic have in his piggy bank?

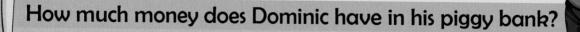

Money is used to pay for things we need or want. Everyone NEEDS:

Food

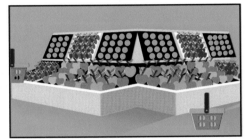

Doctor Visits

Clothes

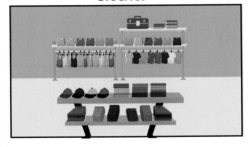

A Place to Live

Mom goes to the grocery store. A cashier takes her money and gives her food. Her family needs food to eat.

Mom goes to the store to buy clothes for the family. They need clothes to wear.

Money is used to pay for things we need or want. These are things we WANT:

Dominic's Mom and Dad wanted new blinds for his room. They gave the woman that makes blinds money and she put them in Dominic's room.

Grant's Mom and Dad wanted a new front porch for his house. They gave the man that builds front porches money and he built one on Grant's house.

al coins and paper bills. You know
lo you get money?

rk For It!

safe.
s.
track of money.
ople healthy.

the picture?

Here are other jobs you might do.

Lawyer. A lawyer fixes things when they are not fair.

Teacher. A teacher helps students to learn.

Scientist. A scientist watches things and tells everyone what they saw.

Engineer. An engineer thinks up a new way of doing something.

Can you match the job with the picture?

Thank you boys, for arranging for your Moms to visit us. Alexis and Jenna, thank you for coming to class today. We appreciate you telling us what you do to earn money.

Thank you, Jenna and Alexis. Class, let's clap our hands to thank them for coming today. Bye, Jenna and Alexis!

Today, you heard what adults do to get money. You don't have to wait until then to earn money to buy things you need or want. Dominic and Grant, would you each please think of three or four things that young people do to earn money?

19

We have learned so much about money today! We learned there are different amounts of money, what it is made of, and what you use it for -- needs and wants. We also learned that you have to earn money and what jobs people do. Thank you for being Great Students!

21

Financial Literacy Will Make Your Child Happier!

Parents and grandparents have high hopes for their children. Some say they want their children to be happy, successful and self-sufficient in life. Other mothers and fathers say they want their children to fulfill their potential, earn enough money to enjoy a comfortable lifestyle and be successful in their career. Will Financial Literacy improve your child's chance for success?

Can Money Buy Happiness?

Is the old phrase, "money can't buy happiness", true? Does a happy, successful adult need to understand finance? Do they need to be financially literate? There have been lots of studies done on the topic. Some say money brings happiness, some say money brings happiness up to a certain income level, some say spending your money strategically brings happiness, and some say money may not bring happiness but it does decrease sadness.

Family Values Should Include Money Matters.

No matter how parents describe their hopes for their children, they must establish the right environment for their goals to be achieved. So where does a parent start? We try to teach our children family values including things like:
--always tell the truth,
--always care about people around you,
--be kind, generous and share,
--take ownership for what you are responsible for and never make excuses,
--be courteous to everyone and never be crude or disrespectful,
--consistently improve yourself and always do the best you can, and
--work hard and show your desire to do well.

Nothing about money is mentioned. If financial literacy makes our children happier (or at least less sad), why don't we teach our children about money matters?

Why Don't We Teach Financial Literacy?

There are a variety of reasons our children are not taught about money matters. First, most parents and teachers don't understand finance. For example, the PwC Educator Survey found: 69% of educators say a lack of qualified teachers is a top challenge of financial education and 67% of educators say they need more professional development for teaching financial education. Second, one of the first things we teach our children is "don't be greedy". Learning about finance is somehow associated with greed and as income inequality grows those who are financially literate are viewed as being greedy. Third, people don't want to learn about finance. Many of the concepts which are taught in finance are contrary to the culture here in America. Finance concepts like "spend less than you make" or in investing, "time is our friend" don't square with today's culture. Our culture is one of impulsive spending and immediate gratification.

Financial Literacy: What You Should Do.

Financial literacy refers to individuals making informed judgments and effective decisions about managing their money. Financial literacy does not mean you have to understand every investment vehicle or every lease versus buy decision. Money matters are not difficult to understand. There are basic concepts that individuals should know in order to enhance their financial decision-making. Those concepts along with a change in behavior could improve the finances of millions of Americans.

Financial "know-how" grows over the course of one's life. The earlier in life these concepts are learned, the better equipped we are to reach our life goals. However, most Americans are not given the opportunity to learn important financial concepts. Both the education system and the parenting process have neglected to develop the appropriate skills needed to succeed in every day life. If you believe financial literacy will make your child happier, what should you do?

First, you must assess your own competency. If you believe you are financially literate and want to help others, you might take the challenge posed by the professional services firm of PwC. PwC's Earn Your Future Curriculum is composed of easy-to-follow lesson plans accompanied by interactive handouts. This curriculum provides students and educators with free and easy access to financial literacy education. The curriculum has certain modules which begin as early as kindergarten. You can download it, teach it, and share it.

If you believe you and your children, no matter your ages, need education to improve your financial decision-making while planning for life events, consider using e-books, webinars or other tools to increase your knowledge base. You won't be sorry you did!

Made in the USA
Lexington, KY
28 February 2019